I0772647
THIS BOOK BELONGS TO

Color Test

12

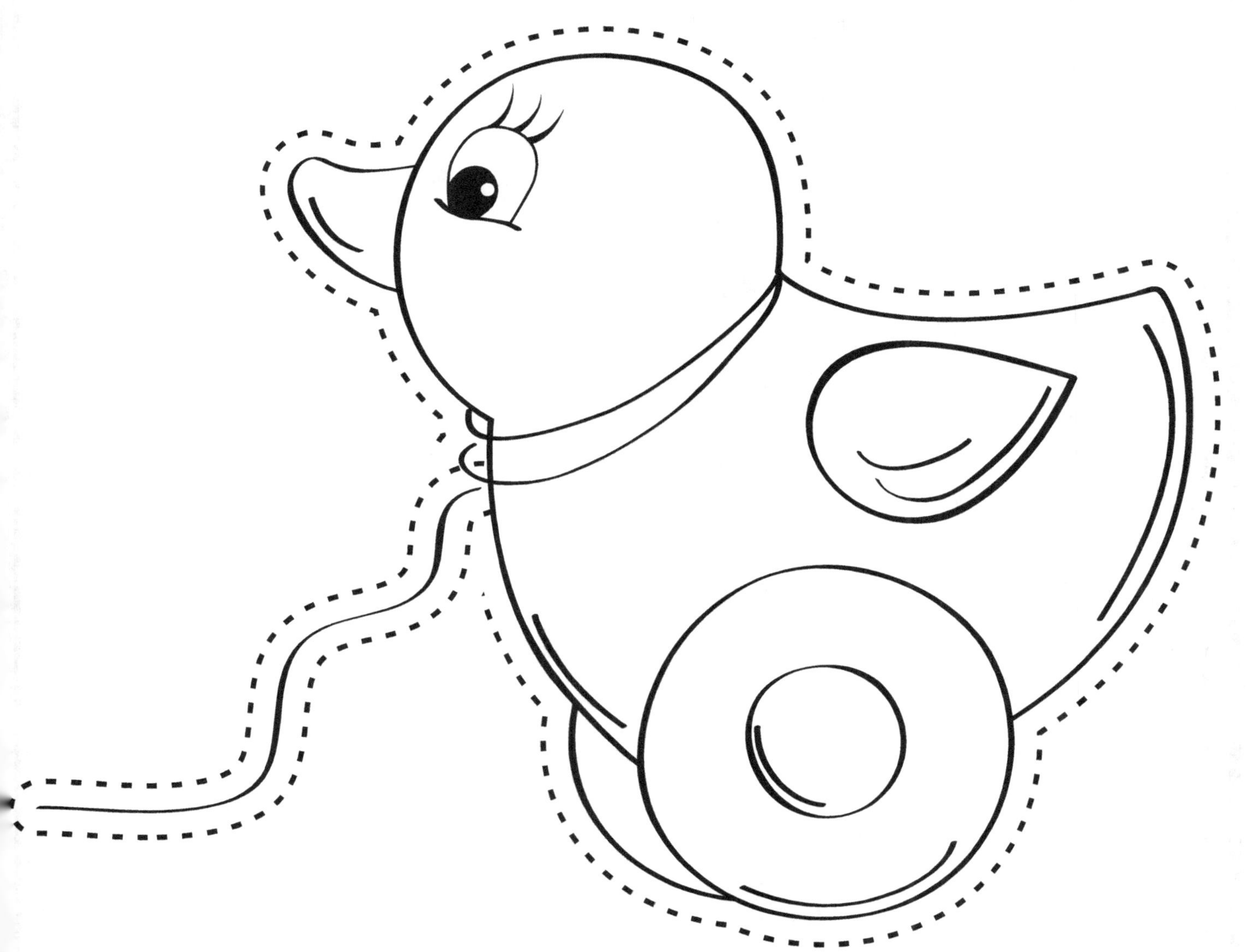

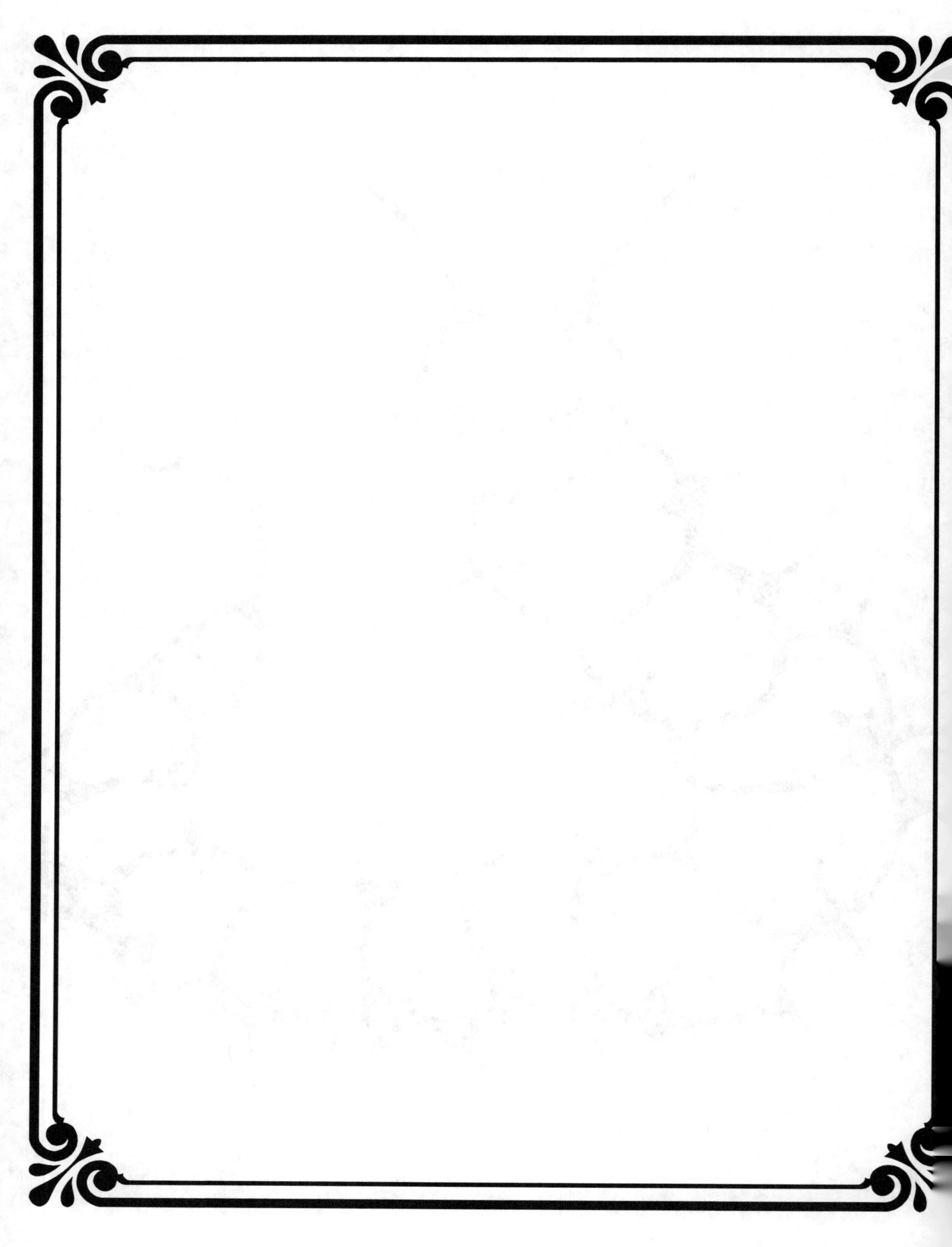

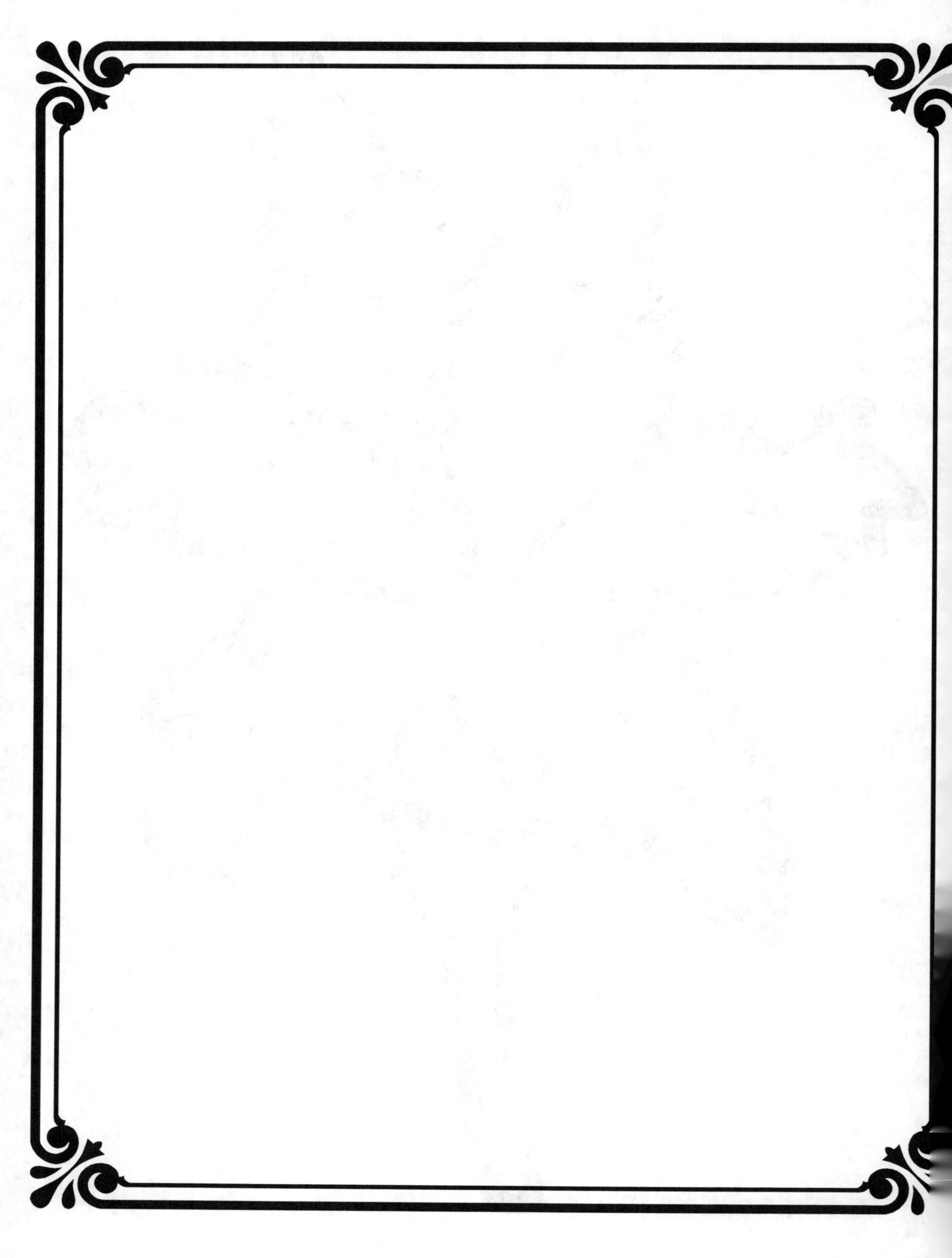

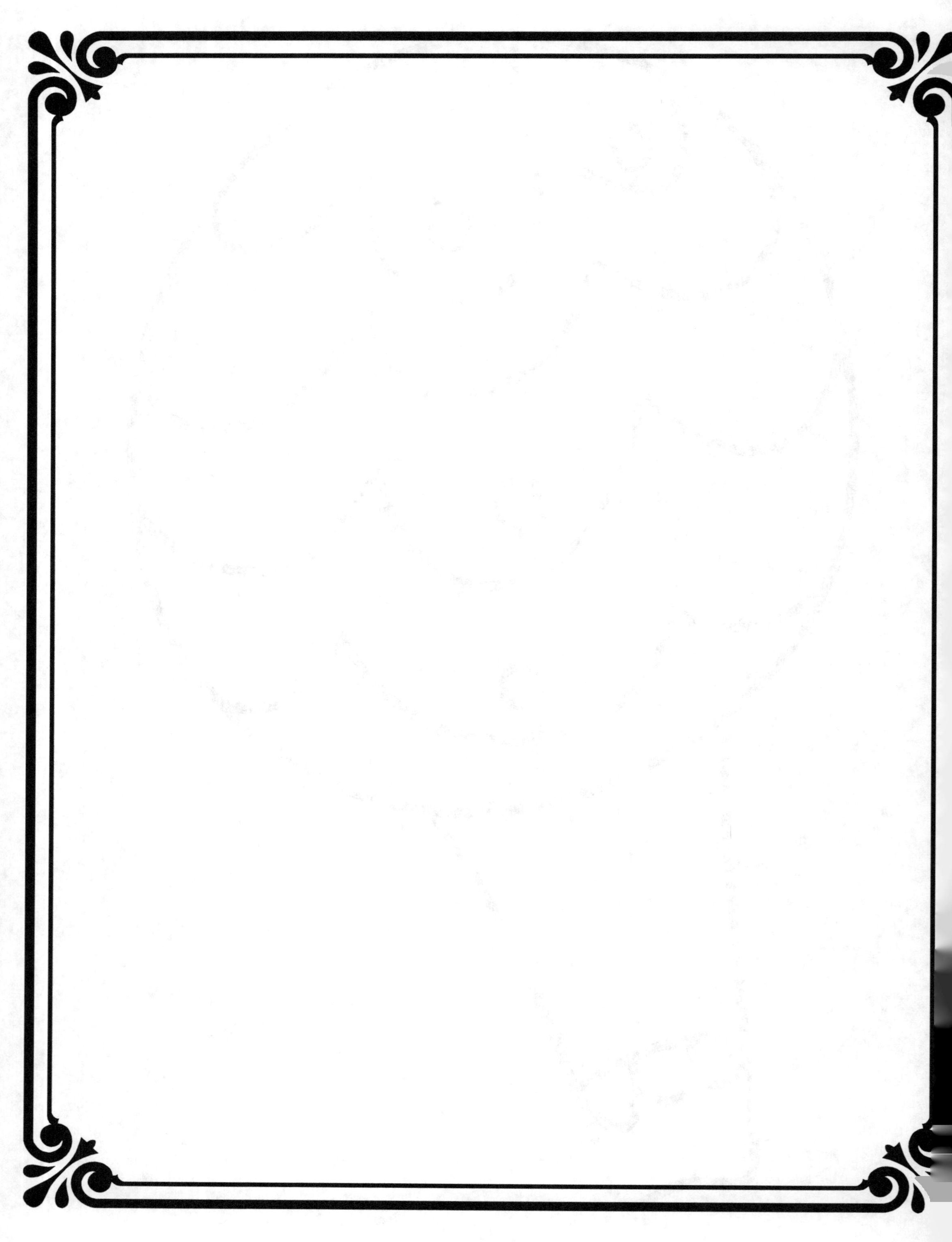

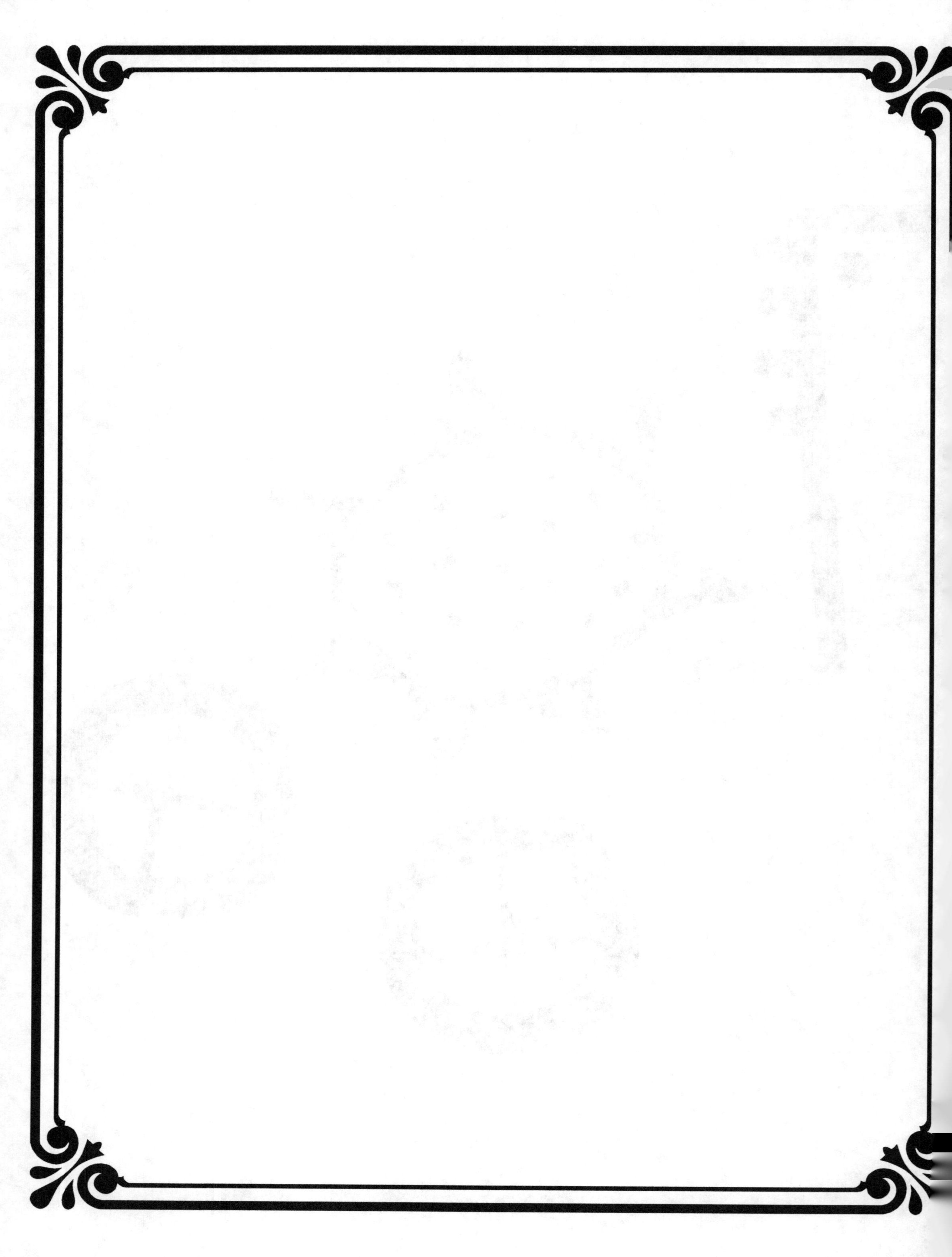

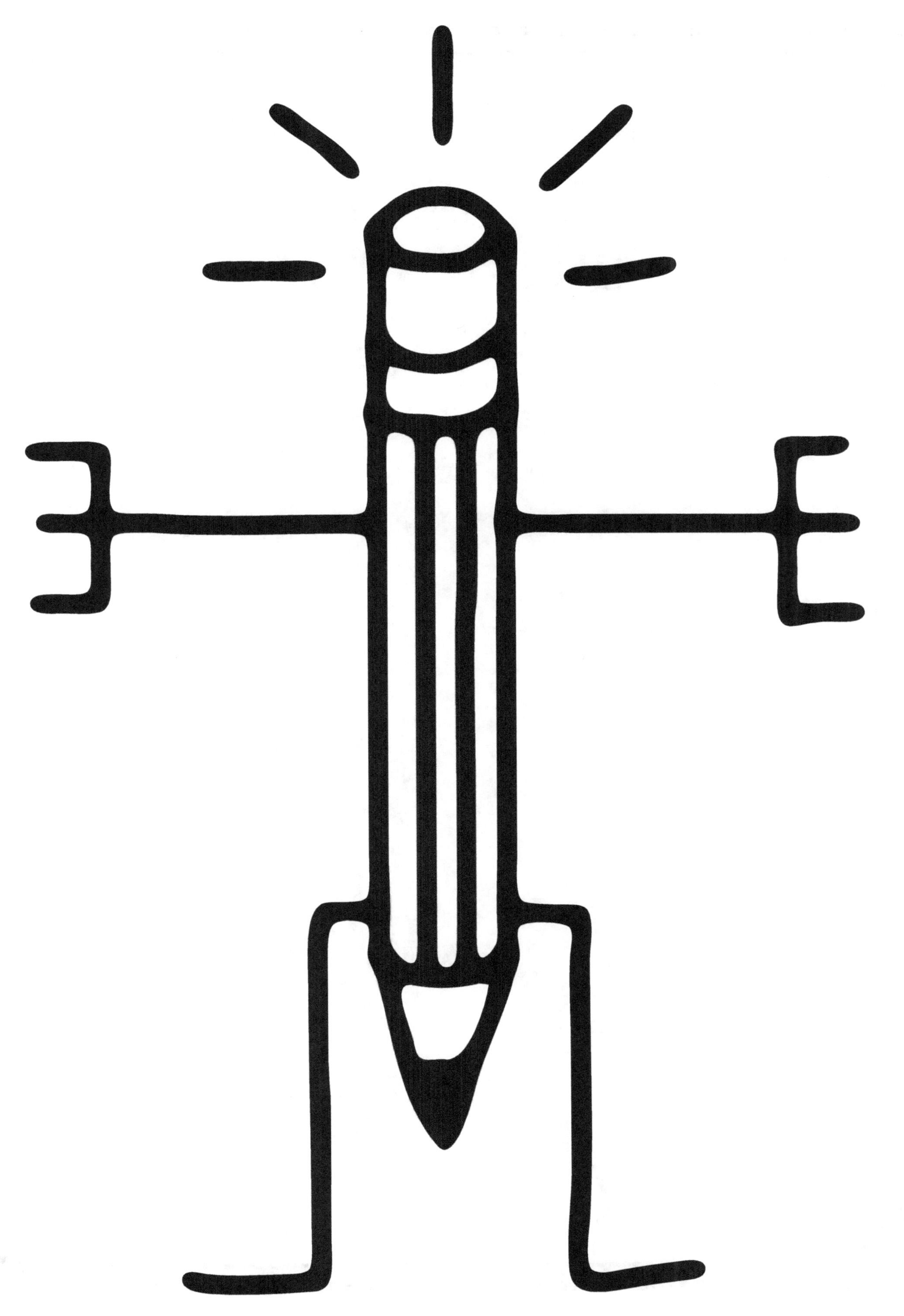

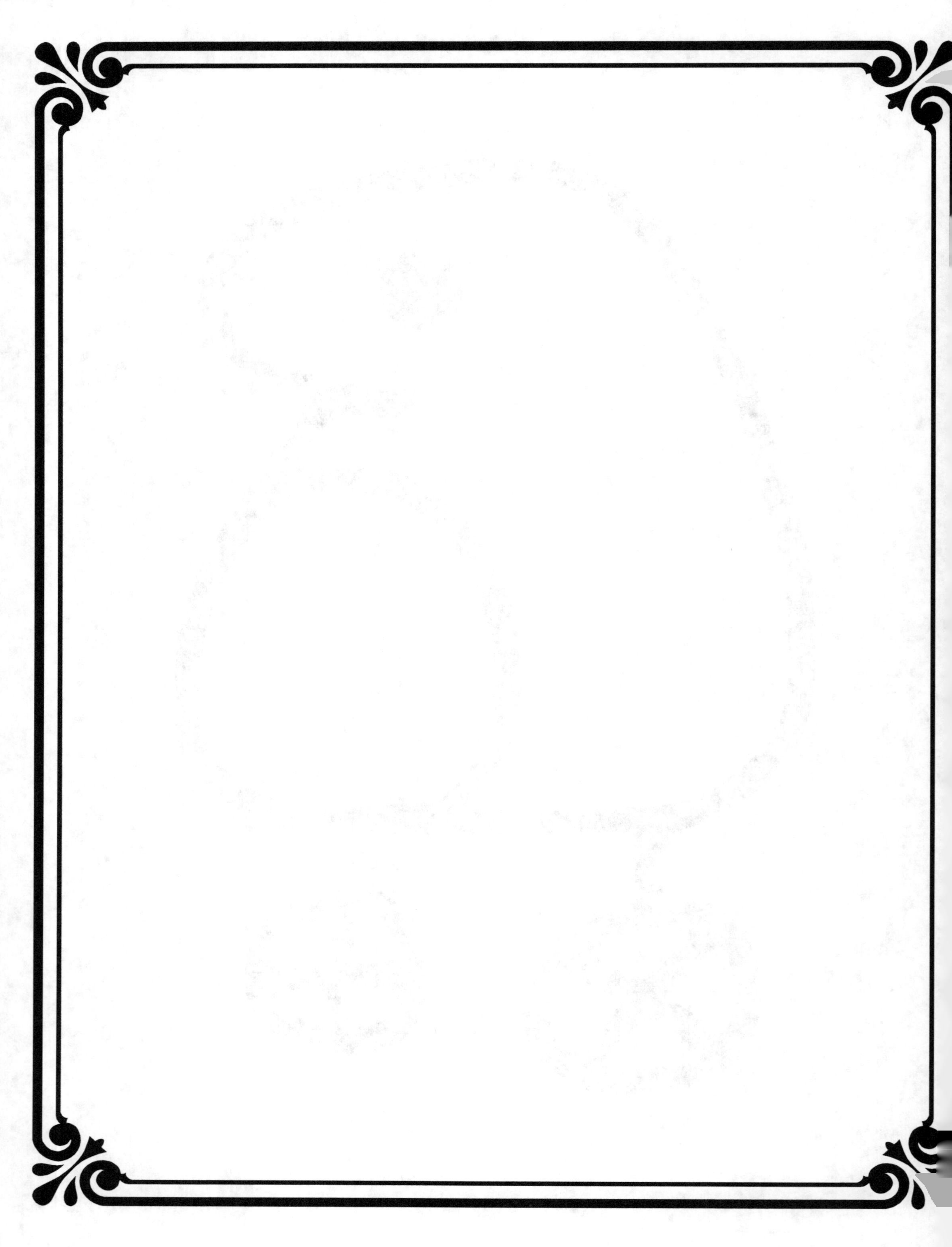

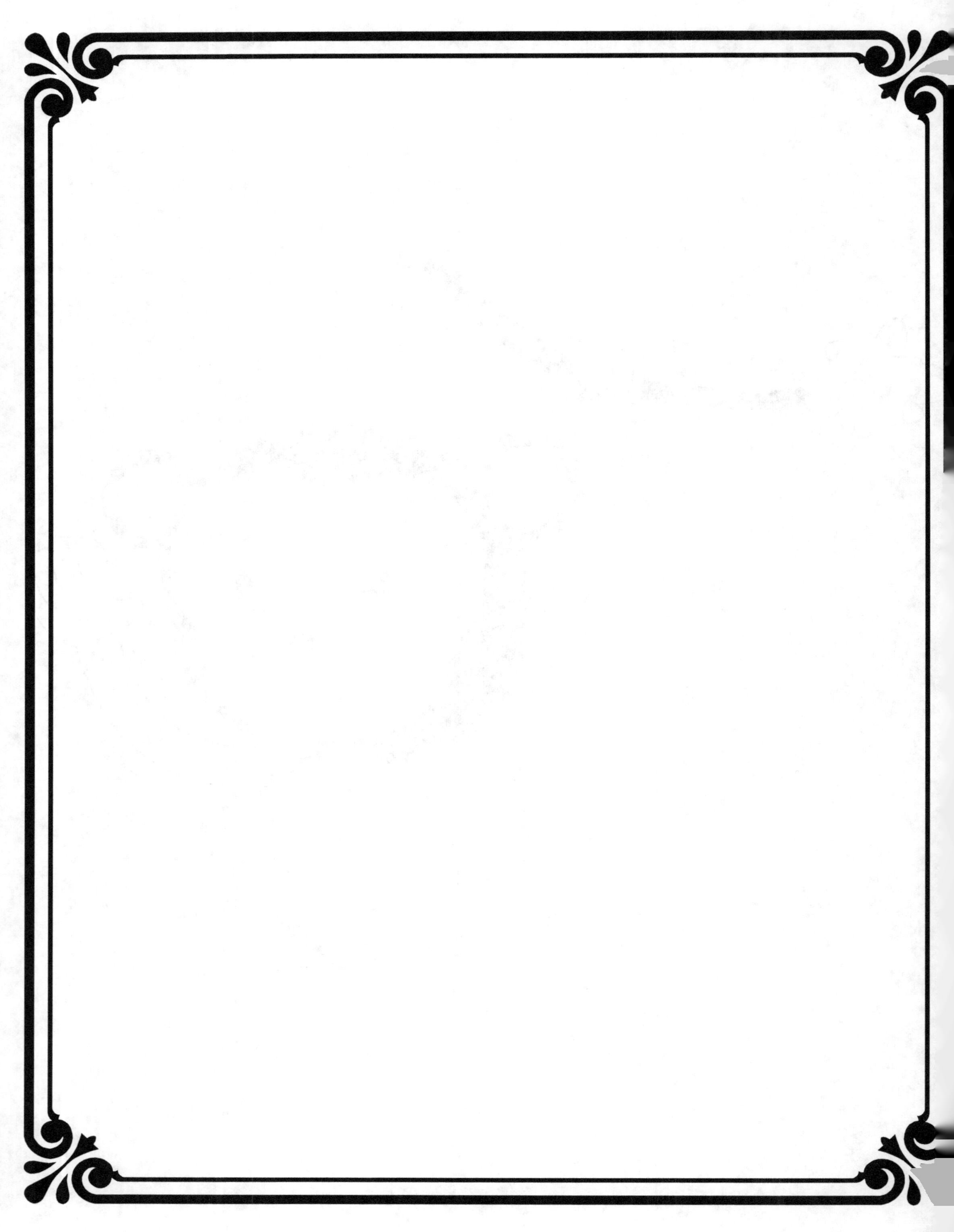